Contents

  Fiction
Crash
page 2

 **Non-fiction**
33 Brave Men
page 18

Written by
David Clayton

Illustrated by
Peter Richardson

Series editor **Dee Reid**

Before reading Crash

Characters

Joe

The lookout

Man in a dark suit

Tricky words

- glowing
- crater
- towards
- carefully
- building
- warehouse
- explosives
- breath

Read these words to the student. Help them with these words when they appear in the text.

Introduction

Joe knew there was something strange going on in Moon City but he didn't know what. He had seen strange lights glowing near the mine outside the city and he decided to check them out. The lights were coming from a sort of warehouse hidden in a crater. People in silver suits were carrying boxes to a moontruck. Joe had to find out what was in the boxes.

Crash

Joe was busy trying to work things out.
He had seen strange lights glowing
near the mine outside Moon City.
What is going on? he thought.
Then he saw a bus taking miners to
the mine. This was his chance to find out.
He got on the bus.

When the bus got to the mine, Joe let all the miners get off first. Then he set off to nose around. Far away he could see a big crater in the ground. There was a strange light coming from it. He checked that nobody was looking, then he ran off towards the light.

As Joe got closer to the light, he could see a man standing at the top of the crater.
He was a lookout.
Why is there a lookout? thought Joe. *And why does he need a gun?*

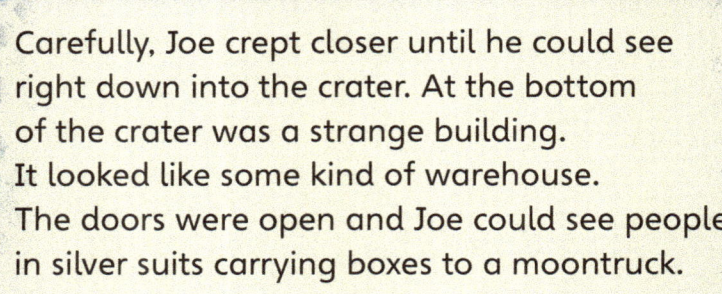

Carefully, Joe crept closer until he could see right down into the crater. At the bottom of the crater was a strange building. It looked like some kind of warehouse. The doors were open and Joe could see people in silver suits carrying boxes to a moontruck.

What could be in the boxes? thought Joe. Then his heart skipped a beat. They were loading explosives on to the moontruck!

The moontruck set off.
Just then Joe's foot slipped and some small stones went crashing down into the crater.
The lookout spun around and Joe ducked quickly behind a rock.

The man moved closer to where Joe was hiding.
Joe held his breath.
At last the man turned and walked away.

Joe's mind was buzzing. *What are the explosives for? Where are they taking them?* There were some buggies parked nearby. Joe jumped in the nearest buggy. He started the engine and set off after the moontruck.

Joe followed the lights from the moontruck. He did not get too close because he did not want to be seen. Then the truck turned and drove straight towards Moon City.

Why are they taking explosives to Moon City? thought Joe.
He turned to get a closer look when…

CRASH! Joe felt the buggy roll over and over and then fall down and down.

Then it came to a sudden stop.
Joe was very shaken.
Slowly he climbed out of the buggy
and crawled on to the roof.

The buggy had crashed down an old mine shaft.
There was no way Joe could climb out on his own.
Nobody knows I'm here! I'll die if I don't get out!
he thought.

Joe thought things couldn't get any worse, when he felt the buggy begin to move.
"Help!" yelled Joe as he clung on.
If it slips down any more that will be the end of me! he thought.

Then Joe heard a noise. It sounded like an engine.
It got louder and louder and then it stopped.
Joe saw a rope coming down towards him.
He grabbed it.
This might be a big mistake, he thought. *I don't know who is at the other end of this rope.*
But as he was slowly pulled up, he heard the buggy slip again and then crash all the way down to the bottom of the mine.

Joe was pulled up to the top of the mine. He saw a man in a dark suit standing next to a buggy. He was holding the rope.
"Get in, quick!" the man snapped. "It's dangerous out here!"
"Who...?" said Joe.
"No questions," said the man.
Joe did as he was told.
The buggy raced off at great speed.

Suddenly, the man stopped the buggy.
They were still quite a way from Moon City.
Joe had a really bad feeling. Was he going
to die after all?
"Get out!" said the man.
"Why?" asked Joe.
"No questions," said the man. "You must not
tell anyone about this."
Then the man got back into the buggy and sped off.

Joe set off on the long walk back to Moon City. His mind was buzzing. *Why were people bringing explosives to Moon City? Who was that strange man?* Joe had a feeling that something bad was happening in Moon City…

Quiz

Text comprehension

Literal comprehension
p3 How did Joe get out to the mine?
p9 Where were the moontrucks taking the explosives?

Inferential comprehension
p4 Why did Joe let all the miners get off the bus first?
p7 Why did Joe hold his breath?
p13 Did Joe make the right decision to grab hold of the rope?

Personal response
- Was Joe wise to get in a buggy and follow the moontruck?
- Would you have grabbed hold of the rope?

Word knowledge

p3 Find a word that means 'unusual'.
p8 Find a phrase that suggests that Joe is thinking hard.
p14 What does the speech verb 'snapped' tell us?

Spelling challenge

Read these words:
together   decided   beginning
Now try to spell them!

Ha! Ha! Ha!

How do you get a baby astronaut to sleep?

You rock-et!

Before reading 33 BRAVE MEN

Find out about

- the 33 miners who were trapped in a mine in Chile.

Tricky words

- cause
- rescue
- decided
- electricity
- worried
- surface
- oxygen
- survived

Read these words to the student. Help them with these words when they appear in the text.

Introduction

In 2010, 33 miners were trapped 700 metres underground in a mine in Chile. The trapped men only had a teaspoon of tuna to eat each day. Rescuers drilled holes to look for the lost men but they could not find them. After 17 days the rescuers found them and the miners were all still alive.

33 BRAVE MEN

Mining is dangerous.
Some mines are very deep. They can be up to 3,000 metres deep.
Sometimes there are rock falls which trap miners underground.
If there has been a rock fall it is very difficult to rescue people. Drilling down to rescue them can cause another rock fall.

On 5th August 2010, there was a rock fall in a gold and copper mine in Chile.
33 miners were trapped 700 metres underground. 700,000 tonnes of rock blocked the mine shaft. Nobody knew if the miners were alive.
The rescuers decided to drill small holes to try to find the trapped men. They knew that the miners had no fresh water and not much food.

The miners had 15 cans of tuna but they did not know how long the food would have to last. At first they each had a teaspoon of tuna every 24 hours. But when the rescuers did not come, they changed it to having a teaspoon every 48 hours and then every 72 hours.

Some of the miners got scared and upset because they were trapped. They did not know if they would ever get out of the mine. However, the miners' boss gave everyone jobs to keep them busy.

For 17 days the rescuers drilled holes to look for the lost men, but they could not find them. Lots of people thought they must be dead. Then, when everyone was beginning to give up hope, a drill broke through to the tunnel where the men were. The rescuers had found the 33 trapped men and they were all alive!

The first drill hole down to the miners was very narrow, so only small things could be sent down to them. The men were sent water, food and letters from home.
Then a phone and a video camera were sent down to them. Now they could talk to their families and the rest of the world could see how they were living. People were shocked to see how thin the miners were.

The drill hole was made wider.
Now more supplies could be sent
down to the miners.
Rescuers sent down an electricity
supply so that the miners could
have lights and a fan to stay cool.
Then they sent down a small TV.
The miners were able to watch
Chile play in a football match.

Some of the men wanted cigarettes and beer. Cigarettes were sent down, but not beer.

Rescuers were worried that beer might make the men start to fight as they had been trapped for so long.

On the surface, a tent village for families and rescuers was set up. It was called Camp Hope. The President of Chile visited the camp to talk to the miners on the phone. News reporters came from all over the world to wait in the camp for the miners to be rescued.

Next, rescuers brought a big drill to make the hole wider. They were worried that it might make more rocks fall. So they had to drill very slowly.
They made a cage to lift the men out. It had a light and oxygen in it. There was only room in the cage for one man at a time. Down below, the men had to stay thin enough to fit in the cage.

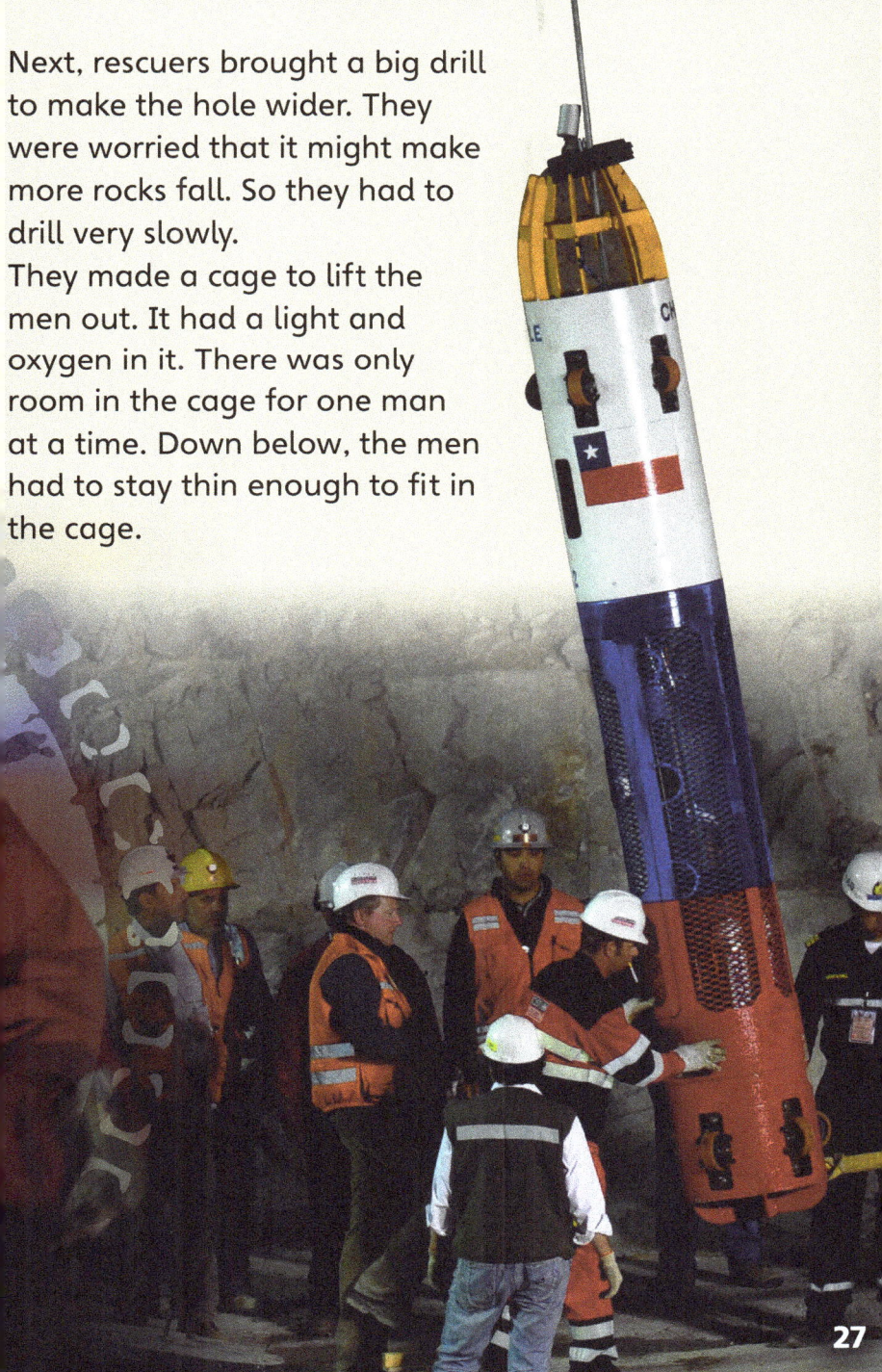

On 17th October 2010, rescuers began to lift the men out of the mine. The fittest men came out first in case the cage got stuck. But there were no problems. It took one hour to lift the first man to the surface. But the rescuers were able to speed things up and it only took 25 minutes for the last man to be lifted out.

The miners had to wear sunglasses as they came out of the mine. They had been in the dark so long that their eyes could not cope with the bright sun.

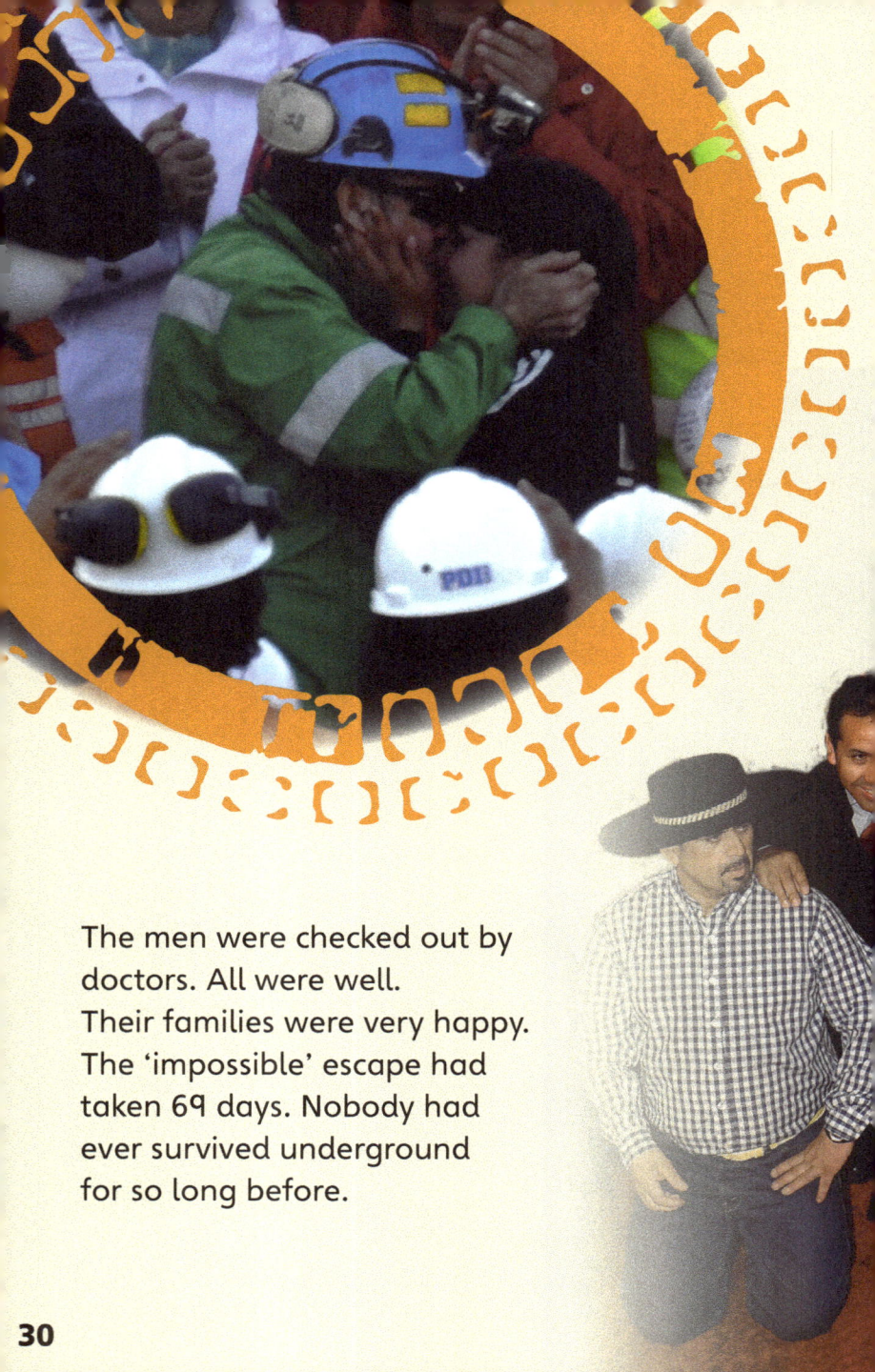

The men were checked out by doctors. All were well. Their families were very happy. The 'impossible' escape had taken 69 days. Nobody had ever survived underground for so long before.

The miners' lives had changed forever. Some of them became famous. Others wanted a quiet life again. But all the men agreed to share any money they got for stories of their time trapped down the mine together.

Quiz

Text comprehension

Literal comprehension

p19 Why is it dangerous to drill down to rescue trapped miners?

p27 Why was it important that the trapped miners stayed thin?

Inferential comprehension

p21 Why did the miners eat less and less tuna each day?

p26 Why do you think the tent village was called Camp Hope?

p28 Why did they send the fittest men in the cage first?

Personal response

- What would be the worst thing about being trapped underground for 69 days?
- Have you ever been trapped anywhere – in a lift or a loo? How did you feel?

Word knowledge

p19 Find a word that means 'very risky'.
p29 Find an adjective on this page.
p30 Why is the word 'impossible' in inverted commas?

Spelling challenge

Read these words:

laughed   bought   anybody

Now try to spell them!

Ha! Ha! Ha!

What gets bigger and bigger as you take more away from it?

A hole!